I0214446

Memories

of my

Father

by

Eric R. Larson

MEMORIES OF MY FATHER.
Copyright © 2020 by Eric R. Larson
All rights reserved.

Except as permitted under the U.S. Copyright Act of 1976, no part
of this publication may be reproduced, distributed, or transmitted
in any form or by any means, or stored in a database or retrieval
system, without prior written permission of the publisher, except
by a reviewer who may quote brief passages in a review.

Direct all inquiries and orders to:
Deep Root Press
4434 Utah St., San Diego, California, 92116 USA
www.deeprootpress.com

Publisher's Cataloging-in-Publication data

Names: Larson, Eric Robert, author.

Title: Memories of my father : fractured conversations on the
nature of manhood /by Eric. R. Larson.

Description: San Diego, CA: Deep Root Press, 2020.

Identifiers: LCCN: 2019911260 | ISBN: 978-0-9828019-6-3

Subjects: LCSH Larson, Eric Robert—Family. | Fathers and sons.
| Sons. | Masculinity. | Men—Family relationships. | Grief. |

BISAC BIOGRAPHY & AUTOBIOGRAPHY / Personal Memoirs
| FAMILY & RELATIONSHIPS / Death, Grief, Bereavement

Classification: LCC HQ1090 .L37 2020 | DDC 305.3/092—dc23

Edited by: Patrick McMahon

Cover & layout design: Anton Khodakovsky

Printed in the United States of America

Memories

of my

Father

by

Eric R. Larson

fractured conversations
on the nature of manhood

DEEP
ROOT
PRESS
SAN DIEGO

Without anger, there is no action

Without fear, there is no courage

Without sadness, there is no joy

*The difference between the mystic
and the madman,*

is that the mystic knows who is listening

Preface

Memories are like butterflies. They come, and they go. They flit about, often in the sun. In these moments, we feel warm inside.

Memories can also be like worms. Things that wriggle in dark places. Things that we do not want to think about. Or remember.

I had a difficult relationship with my father. He was a man I did not understand. After he passed away, memories would pop into my head at the strangest times, both butterflies and worms. I began writing stories to myself, to preserve the memories.

These are memories of my father.

—Eric R. Larson

demons dwell in the smoke of the unspoken

Contents

Prologue

I remember the day my father died. It was a Saturday.

I can remember the moment I heard the news.

I had slept in, not that late, just a lazy Saturday morning after a long week and a Friday night with perhaps one too many.

I heard the buzz of my mobile from the other room. *Hmmm, who's calling this early?* I rolled over, pulled the pillow over my head, tried to go back to sleep. Then the house phone rang. *Damn, somebody wants me.*

I pulled myself out of bed. Checked the voice message. It was from my brother.

"Call me when you get this."

At that point, I knew something was up. I called, got routed to voice mail. Said something. Don't remember exactly what.

I hung up the phone, looked around. Rubbed the sleep from my eyes. Mother nature was calling. I turned toward the door, then grabbed my phone, just in case.

I shuffled to the bathroom, set down the phone, pulled down my pajamas, turned around and sat down, did my thing. I was sitting there, catching my breath, when my mobile buzzed again. I looked at the screen, it was my brother.

Do I take this call?

I hadn't had a chance to . . . wipe, wash, clean, pull myself together. Whatever. I took the call. We bantered for a few seconds, then he said it.

"Dad passed away this morning."

I was literally sitting on the shitter.

Kodak Moment

It's Monday. Two days since I heard the news.

I've been cleaning the closet.

Not just any closet – that closet. The one where you keep things that are close and personal, even though you don't use them every day. I opened one of the boxes my father sent me a few years ago. Papers, photos, service medals, dog tags, a scrap book. Mementos from his military days.

The scrap book was thick. Ivory cover, bound together with string. Heavy pages, yellowed with the passage of time, filled with old photos. Black & white, post card sized, a white border with serrated edges. You know the kind.

I've looked through this scrap book many times. Never read it cover to cover. Probably never will. Today, the pictures seemed different.

I closed the book, dusted off the cover. Put everything in a new box, with a lid that seals. I want to preserve and protect what's inside. I then started cleaning the rest of the closet. Not just the boxes, but the floor, the walls, the shelves, even the closet rod and the coat hangers.

I started thumbing through the clothes, mostly outerwear, coats and jackets.

One of the coats was a warm up jacket from Land's End. Nylon shell, with a fleece liner. Years ago, my dad and stepmom had sent it as a Christmas gift. I don't use it much anymore, the zipper is broken. I've been meaning to write Land's End to get it fixed. Supposedly, they offer a lifetime guarantee. I wonder if that meant my lifetime? Or his?

On the shelf above were other boxes, some filled with slides. The slides are in carousels, circular trays that allow you to show your slides in a projector, going forward and backward as often as you wish. I have carousels of various cross-country trips I have taken, in cars, or on a bicycle.

I opened one of the boxes. A hand written label. West Coast Trip 1983. I always wanted to show these slides to my father. If he ever came to visit.

Printed on each slide, in red, yellow, and blue:

Ektachrome. Processed by Kodak.

Slides in a carousel. In a box. With a lid. On a shelf. In a closet. Above the floor where I keep a scrapbook from my father.

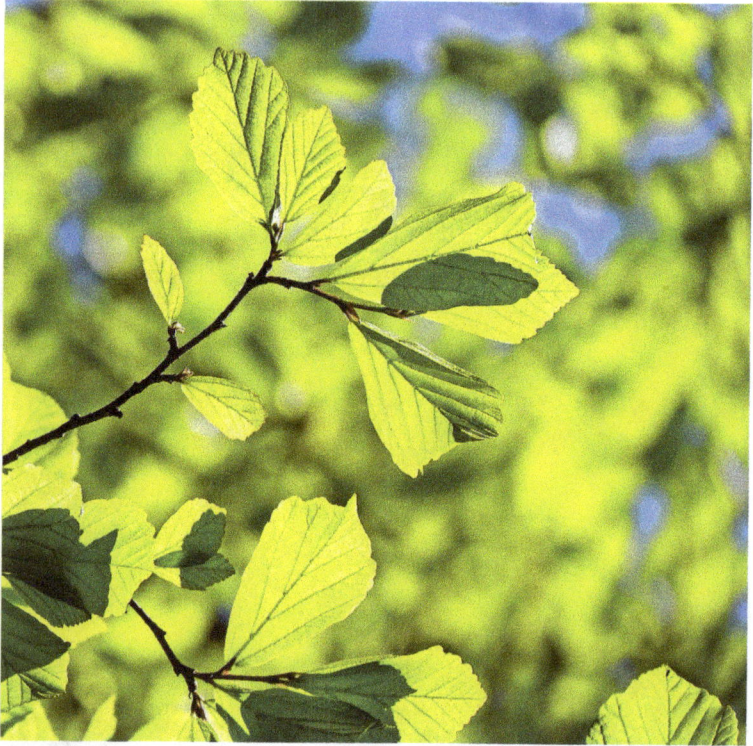

Little Flags

My father was born in 1930. It was a long time ago. It was a different place, a different world, a different time. It was a world of clear choices, between black and white, good and bad, right and wrong.

I remember the day my brother and I went to get some poles. Our dad was building a new dock on his new house on the lake. Work was being done on the dam, so the lake water was low. A good time for maintenance. So we went to get some poles. Old telephone poles, coated with creosote. Perfect for a dock, on a house, on a lake.

On our way back, somewhere between a dip and a curve, I lost control. I was going a little too fast on a winding country road, in a place not my own. The truck skidded one way, the trailer skidded another. The word yonder comes to mind.

A few seconds later, there were poles everywhere, scattered like toothpicks across a floor. Like a scene from the movie *Rain Man.*

82. 82. 82.

I don't remember counting the poles, just cringing, laughing, saying something like *Holy Shit,* and then scrambling to get the poles off the road, back in the trailer, out of harm's way.

It was a different place, a different world, a different time.

Today, we live in the present, in the here and now. We have places to go. Things we need to do. Today, we move on, quickly and quietly. We are fast. We are efficient. We have no time for stories, especially stories told by old men. In our efficiency, things leak out.

"Hey asshole!" Get the < insert nasty comment 1 > out of my way! What the < insert nasty comment 2 > is wrong with you?"

Sorry, I didn't mean to cause any trouble. I am having a bad day. My father just died. Please forgive me.

I remember going to funerals, when I was little. I didn't understand what was going on.

I remember dressing up nice, going to church, not on a Sunday, then walking outside, seeing the cars lined up, all in a row. People moving silently, nobody talking, cars driving away, one after the other. A long, slow drive. A little flag on each car, flapping in the wind.

Thup. Thup. Thup. Thup. Thup.

Afterwards, we would stand around looking at each other, wondering what to say.

Somehow, it seemed like the right thing to do.

It was a different place, a different world, a different time.

Good Deal

It's a simple question, one we often ask our friends.

Did you get a good deal?

Growing up, my father always stressed the importance of getting a good deal. *Be careful with your money,* he used to say. *Money doesn't grow on trees.*

Sometimes, he would come home with something he bought. Sometimes new, sometimes used. Usually it was something useful, even cool. On occasion it was something weird. Really weird.

I found this at a garage sale. I got a good deal.

For years, for decades, I based purchasing decisions on this premise. It affected almost every decision I made. The things I bought, the clothes I wore, the car I drove, the woman I dated.

Sometimes, I bought things I didn't really want, or didn't need. In the back of my head, there was always a little voice asking:

Did you get a good deal?

I know what you're thinking. Those are just words, spoken by an old man.

> *"When I was your age, we used to walk 14*
> *miles to school, through cold winds and*
> *drifting snow, and we were happy about it!"*

Truth be told, it's not my father's fault. He was born in a different place, in a different time. He grew up counting pennies, counting nickels, saving dimes. He lived through a war to end all wars, and served in another.

Several years ago, I finished a big project. I decided to buy myself something, as a reward. I settled on a new flat screen TV. I didn't need all the bells and whistles, just a good TV with with a great picture.

I shopped around, comparing makes and models, prices, features. I went to my local electronics store, to see things in person. The experience was overhwelming.

There were televisions of every make and model, in every size you could think of, with features all over the map. HD. LED. OLED. QLED. 4K Ultra. HDR. WTF.

In one aisle, there were televisions from Sony. I know the display was carefully organized to impress. There were features, benefits, warranties, promises. I don't remember the details. I do remember the picture was breathtaking. And it was expensive.

I walked past that aisle, past the other premium brands, to the discount aisle. Discontinued models, floor samples, second tier brands.

I kept walking back to the Sony display, comparing features, benefits, picture quality, price.

I settled on an off-brand TV, heavily discounted. I told the sales rep, *I'll take this one.* It was a good deal.

We walked up to the register, and started the check out process. We went through the details, price, taxes, warranty, etc. The sales rep handed me a pen, to sign on the dotted line.

You know what, I changed my mind. I'll take the Sony.

I took it home, set it up. I still have it today.

Did I get a good deal? Maybe. Maybe not. I got what I wanted.

To this day, my younger brother still uses the phrase. As an expression. As a greeting. As a good-bye. I don't know if he realizes it. But every time we talk, he says it.

Good Deal.

I love it when he says that. It makes me feel good. Every time.

Feeling Shitty

A song has been in my head today. Actually, not a song, just some lyrics.

I feel pretty, oh so pretty,

I feel witty and happy and bright!

I don't remember where it was from, who wrote it. Some musical, from days long ago. You remember musicals, don't you? Those old movies with beautiful people, singing and dancing, happy as could be. If only real life was like that.

The song in my head could have been from a Disney movie. Or maybe a Rodgers and Hammerstein musical. Or the Rogers, Totally Hammered.

In any event, that song has been in and out of my head all day today. All god damn day. Except in my head, the lyrics have been a bit different.

In my head, the words go something like this:

I feel shitty, oh so shitty,

I feel petty and angry and fight!

No need to say, I have been in a funk this week. And everybody seems to have noticed.

Crazy homeless people see me coming, and they run the other way. Pit bulls quiver in fear. Friends pat me on the arm, gently. *If you ever need to talk, give me a call.* I say thanks, then watch them out of the corner of my eye, as they walk away. I see their glances at each other, the way they roll their eyes, the words they form to each other, without speaking.

Yes, I am in a bad space. Some might call it a funk.

Yes, I am angry and hurt and I can't see straight. Deal with it.

My father just died. And that sucks. It really sucks.

Right now, I am not interested in hearing condolences, or in sharing a Kodak Moment, or in reading a fairy tale with a *They All Lived Happily Ever After* ending.

I don't want to watch any movies with beautiful people, singing and dancing, happy as can be.

And I sure as hell don't feel like singing in the rain.

I just feel shitty.

Guilty Dogs

Growing up, we always had pets of one kind or another. Usually cats, but also turtles, chameleons, hamsters, gerbils, tropical fish, even a few snakes.

When I was in high school, we got our first dog. Not just any dog, we went all in. We got a Saint Bernard. Her name was Brandy. She was the runt of her litter. Fully grown, she topped out at about 100 pounds. A runt. But a wonderful dog.

When my parents divorced, Brandy went with Dad. While she wasn't *his dog*, it made sense. She was a big dog, and needed space, and food. My dad re-married, and moved away. He settled in Alabama, outside of Tuscaloosa, in a small house on a lake. In time, Brandy passed away. They got a new dog, another Saint Bernard, and then a few more. Big dogs don't live very long, but they live big lives.

One year, I visited my father for Thanksgiving, along with my older brother. There were plans for a great feast. Early in the morning, my stepmother threw a couple of turkeys on the smoker. I'd never had smoked turkey before. I was looking forward to it.

We set off on errands, and some fun. I think my brother and I even played a round of golf with my dad. When we got back to the house, the dogs met us. They were happy to see us, as always. But their mannerisms seemed different. As if they were guilty of something.

A few minutes later, we went into the garage. The dogs followed, tails wagging, tongues hanging out. They seemed so happy.

In the garage, the smoker was on its side, the lid a few feet away. The turkeys were gone – and I mean gone. There was no meat to be found. No bones. No skin. Nothing. The dogs had eaten *everything*.

My dad was furious. I thought it was hilarious.

My stepmother ended up cooking something else for Thanksgiving dinner. I don't remember exactly what, I think it was ham.

I do remember it was delicious.

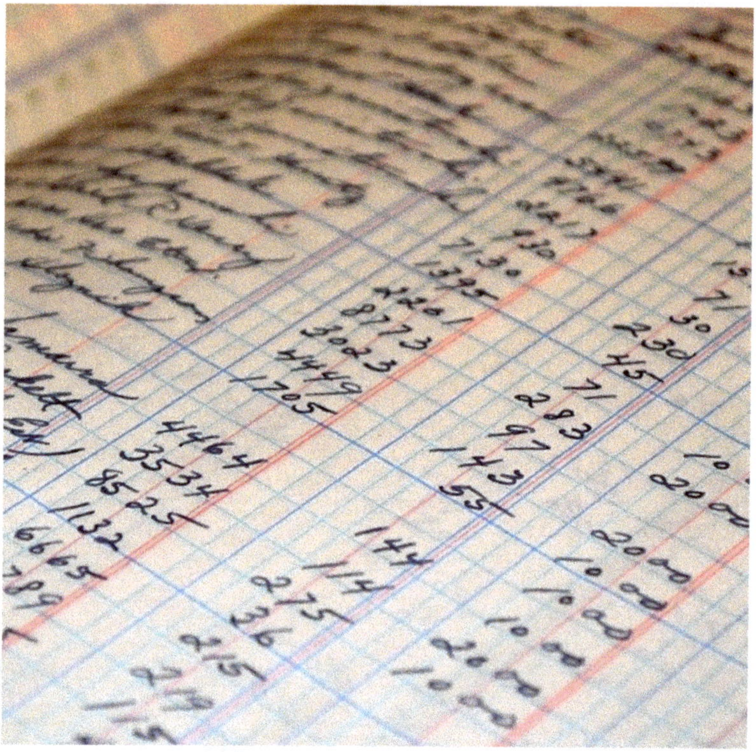

The Ledger

I remember that first ledger. It was a small book, with a black cover and a red spine. Inside, ivory colored pages with columns and lines. Something you might buy at a stationery store, for keeping track of things.

My father started the ledger. He was trying to teach me something. I didn't understand at the time.

I don't remember the how and why, but I wanted my own set of golf clubs. I might have been 10. I didn't have any money. Maybe some nickels and dimes, and a dollar bill here and there. Not enough to matter.

My dad offered to loan me some money. But I would have to pay it back over time. We settled on $20. He gave me the bills. Crisp and green.

I started looking for some clubs to buy; garage sales, want ads in the paper. I found a set. A bag, some clubs, a putter, some golf balls and tees. I was so excited.

My dad went with me to help with the purchase. I came home with a set of clubs that were mine. They were no longer borrowed, or left over. They were mine. Except, I still needed to pay for them. So my dad used a ledger.

He made an entry at the top of the page. A description of the purchase, with the date, the price, and the amount to be financed. The lettering crisp and precise.

Each month, I would make a payment, and he would update the ledger. Each entry with the date, the payment amount, and the balance. *Amount still owed.* The lettering crisp and precise. An agreement between men.

Over time, I paid off the balance. I don't remember how long it took. I do remember how good it felt to see the number zero.

My father closed the ledger, stood up, and shook my hand.

I think I was 11.

Father's Day

It's the second Sunday in June.

Things are green and growing. The days have been getting longer. Mornings are pleasant, evenings tease with subtle promises.

Today is Father's Day.

I think of my father of course. Thoughts, memories, feelings; all flowing thicker than water.

I think of other men in my life, who went tag-teaming with dad. Teachers, coaches, counselors, janitors. Men who stood by me, with me, behind me. Men who had my back. Men who wiped my ass when I was covered in shit.

I think of my brothers. Proud fathers, raising their sons as best as they can. My nephews, far away. I am their uncle, rarely seen.

I think of the uncles in my life. Uncles near and far. Men who made a difference to me. Men with unspoken words, hidden joys, and their own subtle scars. Some I thanked; some I never noticed.

Thoughts flow, manly thoughts, one after the other, details forgotten, sound bites flickering like fireflies on a mental ticker tape.

Thoughts, mixed with questions. Questions unspoken. Questions unasked. What if? Why not? *Because.*

We may not talk much.

That doesn't mean we don't feel.

Happy Father's Day.

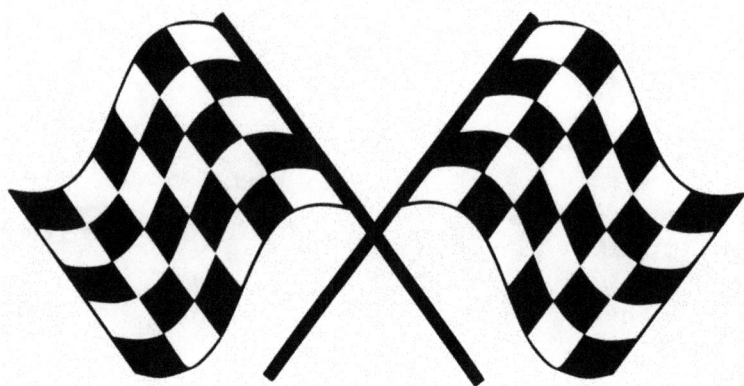

Indy 500

My father was a working man, from a working class family. The men in his family were machinists, toolmakers, miners of iron and copper. Men who worked with their hands. Men who worked with tools. Men with calluses.

My mother also came from a working class family. The men in her family were coal miners and bricklayers. Men with different tools, and different kinds of calluses. Men with a deep sense of pride.

My father worked for Ford Motor Company, ever since he got out of the service. I didn't know what he did, but I remember he went to night school, and studied drafting. He used his hands to make drawings.

He later got a job in the quality department. I know he wrote reports. He used to joke, *I am a quality guy.*

In 1972, when I was 14, a vendor invited him to the Indianapolis 500, *The Greatest Spectacle in Racing*. We went as a family; my father, my mother, my older brother, and I. We stayed at a hotel some 60 miles from the race track.

We got up at the crack of dawn, and made our way to the event. We parked miles away, and walked to the speedway, the crowd and the excitement building as we got closer and closer.

We walked around the infield. There were rows of convertibles filled with celebrities, getting ready for the pre-race festivities. There was Marty Allen, with his fuzzy hair and crazy eyes. And Linda Vaughn, Miss Hurst Golden Shifter. *Va-voom*. As a boy of 14, you remember these things. We headed to our seats.

We had tickets in the main grandstand, across from pit row. Not high enough to see much, but low enough to feel everything. I could look up at the rows above us, and see people everywhere. More people than I ever saw in one place - before, or since.

I could see the curve of the grandstands to the left, wrapped around turn 4. I could see the curve of the grandstand to the right, wrapped around turn 1. And I could see the starting pole, jutting skyward like a beacon.

Next was Jim Nabors, singing *Back Home in Indiana*. I have tears in my eyes with the memory. Then the immortal words *Gentleman, start your engines*. And the roar began.

Every year, I watch the race, and I think about 1972. I can hear the roar of the crowd. I can feel the roar of the engines.

Mario Andretti. Al Unser. Roger Penske. Jim Nabors. Linda Vaughn. Indianapolis.

Whenever I hear these names, I think about 1972.

And I remember my father.

He was a quality guy.

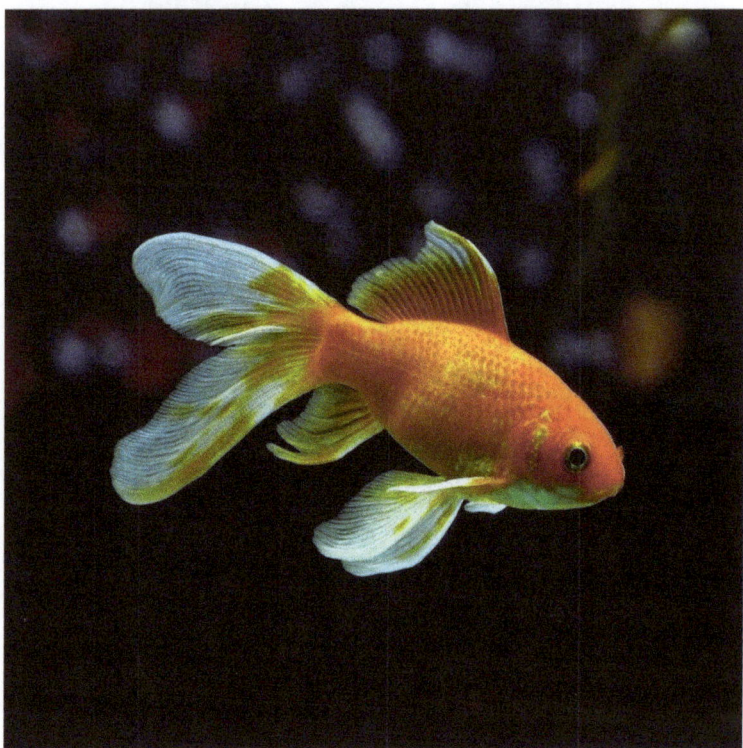

Animals

When I was really young, we had goldfish. They were not pets, but they were something alive, in the house, that we all cared for.

Our first real pet was a cat. Hoppy. We named him that because of the way he jumped. He looked like a bunny rabbit, hopping along.

Growing up, we often went to the zoo. I remember the animals, large and small. The sounds. The smells. The sense of awe and wonder.

When I was old enough, my parents let me have an aquarium. With real tropical fish. I even had a pet snake, for a while.

My siblings had pets of their own: hamsters, gerbils, a ferret. Cute little critters, each with their own quirks, and responsibilties.

When I was in high school, we got a dog. A big dog. A Saint Bernard. She was a bundle of joy and energy and happiness and warmth, all at once.

She also came with a new set of responsibilities. Feeding her. Walking her. Brushing her. Cleaning up after her.

Growing up, there were always animals outside too. Either in our back yard, or Grandpa's back yard. Or in the back yard of a cottage up north, in the woods.

Birds. Squirrels. Snakes. Racoons. Possum. Skunks. Deer. Bear. They were wild creatures. To respect and admire. Sometimes to eat.

Yes, my father was a hunter, and a fisherman. There were guns and trophies. Dead animals, mounted on the wall. Along with pictures and stories. Celebrations of a bountiful harvest. Food for the family.

But there was also something else. A connection to the natural world. It is a relationship that is hard to explain in words.

I rarely understood my father. Yet despite all of our arguments and fights, I never saw him abuse an animal. It just wasn't in him. He was a different man around animals.

I think there was something in that about being out doors. The sound of thunder. The smell of the rain. Hearing – feeling - the wind whispering hello.

Animals can sense weakness and fear. They can feel pain. As well as safety and warmth.

The comfort you feel, when you are in pain and an animal crawls up next to you, and lays its head on your lap.

My father gave me a love for animals.

It is a gift I cherish.

Promise

I don't remember how the fight started, or what it was about. An argument about nothing, that had somehow turned physical. My father had gotten angry, and hit my older brother. It wasn't the first time he had hit one of us, but it was going to be the last.

My older brother was three years ahead of me. Even though he was older, it seemed he was always smaller than I was. Growing up we fought a lot, about anything and everything. While we don't fight anymore, we still don't understand each other.

When my brother got to high school he took up wrestling. I don't remember why. I am sure it provided him an outlet. It also made him strong. Even though he was smaller, I always knew he could kick my ass.

But on that day, when the fight started, I don't think my father realized how strong my brother was. Truth be told, neither did I.

Right after my father hit him, my brother grabbed him, and took him down, right there in the middle of the living room. There weren't a whole lot of words, just a lot of heavy breathing. It wasn't really a fight, but they weren't playing. They were wrestling, one on one. *Mano e mano.* The end came pretty quick.

Stop, I give up.

This time it was my father who had said it. My brother had him pinned. It might have been an arm behind the back, an elbow on his neck, I really don't remember.

I do remember my father whimpering.

Stop, let me up. You're hurting me.

My brother wouldn't let him go. "Promise me you'll never hit us again." My father whimpered again.

Let me up, let me up.

My brother said it again, this time a little but louder.

"Promise me you'll never hit us again."

" PROMISE ! "

He gave my father one more squeeze for emphasis.

I promise.

My brother let my father go. They got up, looked at each other. Two alpha males, sizing each other up. And then slowly backing away.

My father kept his promise, and he never hit any of us again.

My only regret, I never thanked my brother.

Uncle

It is a simple word, used to describe the brother of a parent. Traditionally, it has been a term of respect, and a statement of kinship.

I had – and still have - uncles. The brother of my father. The husband of my father's sister. Brothers of my mother. Husbands of my mother's sisters.

There was my Uncle Gerry. My father's brother. Youngest of his clan. For some thirty years we had no contact, after my father got angry at the reading of his father's will. I have since re-connected with him. I enjoy his stories. He's the one who told me what the word *Detroit* means. I think I was 50.

There was my Uncle *what's his name*. Husband of my father's sister. He disappeared from my life – as did everyone in their family – after that reading of the will.

There were my mother's brothers. I saw them from time to time, at family outings. I don't think she liked them very much.

There were the husbands of my mother's younger sister. Several. I did not know them well.

There was my Uncle Roger. The husband of my mother's older sister. He was a quiet man, with a scar on his chin, from the war. He loved his children. I knew he served his country, but it wasn't until his funeral that I fully understood that service. There was an honor guard, at the cemetary where he was laid to rest.

> *On behalf of the President of the United States, the United States Army, and a grateful nation, please accept this flag as a symbol of our appreciation for your loved one's honorable and faithful service.*

My uncles were men I grew up with, but never really knew. Most with wives and children. Patriachs in their own right. Men who represented *manhood*.

Today, the term uncle is rarely used with respect. We joke about uncles. The crazy uncle. The drunk uncle. Caricatures of men, tossed aside.

Uncle Tom. The passive, spineless one. Uncle Fester. The screwball with no hair.

When did saying uncle become a statement of defeat?

I was born and raised in Michigan. I grew up in a little town in the suburbs of the Detroit - or as I sometimes call it, *day-twah*.

Detroit was, and some would say still is, The Motor City. My father worked for Ford Motor Company in *day-twah*, as did his father, and his brother, and all of my aunts and all of my uncles. I was actually born in Henry Ford Hospital in downtown Detroit – as were all of my siblings and all of my cousins. (Sometimes, we even joked about it. We would ask each other, *What floor were you born on?* as if one floor was better than another).

After I graduated from college I moved away from Michigan. In the years since then – or should I say the decades since then - I have moved around the country, chasing dreams, following the lure of steady employment. And I lost contact with my uncles.

There was a tool chest that my father used to have. It was built by my father's uncle, Uncle Al. I have faint memories of him. I remember he had a thick moustache and a soft smile, and loved fishing, hunting, and a good drink at the end of the day. I also remember he was my father's favorite uncle.

Some thirty years ago I tracked that tool chest down. It had been in Uncle Al's garage, then my dad had it, then my older brother, and then I came across it. I spent some time restoring it. I tore it down to the basics, and rebuilt it piece by piece. The case itself is made of mahogany, and the drawers are all solid wood, with maple front pieces. The fittings are all brass (some original, some replacements), and the original front lock is intact.

While I do not have the provenance, it is a family heirloom that I treasure. A gift from an uncle.

I am an uncle.

I have nieces and nephews, children of my siblings. They all live far away. I visit as often as I can. I write, I call, I send them cards on special occasions.

I wonder what impact I have made on their lives, because I really don't know. They never call, they rarely write. But I am still their uncle.

I sometimes wonder what they say about me.

The Roof

I grew up in the suburbs. We lived on a quiet street, in a small house with a big yard.

It was a place of magic and mystery, filled with secret spaces. The garage. The wood pile. The empty lot next door. The woods at the bottom of the hill. The crawl space under the house. The roof. They were places to play hide and seek. And places to just hide.

Like many houses, it had a front door in the middle of the house, one that opened into the front foyer. The front door was big and bulky, and hard to get to. So it was rarely used.

Instead, we used a side door. That door opened directly from the dining room to the driveway, via a covered patio. So you could park in the driveway, walk through the covered patio, knock on the side door, and then come into the house. It was the way most people came and went, especially friends and family.

On the outside of the patio there were a couple of steps. On each side a pedestal, made of bricks and mortar, with a square concrete top. You could set a flower pot on each pedestal, or a piece of sculpture. Something to celebrate an arrival to the house. Except we never did.

The most interesting thing about these pedestals was that they offered easy access to the roof. If you were nimble, you could jump from the front steps to the top of the pedestal, and then slide your butt on to the roof of the patio. From there, you could walk onto the roof of the house. From the roof, you could see – and hear – anything and everything that was going on.

Growing up, my father and I often argued, and I mean *argued.* We would yell and scream and do everything but hit each other – and sometimes that too.

In our arguments, I would sometimes threaten to run away. My father would laugh, and taunt me. *Where do you think you are going to go?* he used to say.

Deep inside, I knew he was right.

So I would go and find a place to hide. A place somewhere outside. I wanted to be any where but in that house. His house.

One of the places I learned to hide was the roof. I knew how to get there quickly and quietly, and I knew the places where no one could see me. From there I could listen to my parents argue, and hear them calling my name. While I was hiding.

I would stay there on the roof for hours, angry and upset, scared and confused. Sometimes I would sulk, sometimes I would cry. But mostly, I just hid. It was a game of sorts, hide and seek for the teenage years. But it was no longer a child's game. And there was no way for me to win.

Eventually, the chaos would subside, the sun would go down, and I would fall asleep. On the roof.

Sometime during the night, I would wake up. Perhaps it was from the cold, or from hearing my parents calling out my name.

I would then come down from the roof, first to one of the concrete pedestals, then to the front steps of the patio.

Then, I would open the patio door, slowly, gently, quietly, and close it behind me. Then, a few steps to the side door. It was a big heavy door, with big heavy knob, but almost always unlocked. A slow turn and a soft push, and I would then be in the dining room. I'd then close the door behind me, locking it as quietly as I could.

I'd tiptoe across the living room, then down the hall. I'd slip into my room and crawl into bed, careful not to wake my brothers.

As quiet as I thought I was, my father would always hear me come in.

He would open the bedroom door, and call my name.

"Is that you?"

Yeah.

There would be silence – seconds, minutes, lifetimes.

Then, I would hear his voice, kind and loving.

"Go to sleep."

In the morning, everything would be cheerful and pleasant, as if nothing unusual had ever happened.

We never talked about those nights.

The Apron

She stood on the porch, glaring at me. *What is it this time?*

I was living in Big Sur. I had been recovering from a head injury. The physical wounds had healed, but recent life events had triggered all kinds of issues, and I was working through them. Having my answers questioned.

I had been to the Esalen Institute many times, taking workshops, getting bodywork, even doing a stint as a work scholar. During my visits I had gotten to know some of the people who lived in Big Sur. One of them had suggested I move there for a while, to work through things. She invited me to be her roommate, to share expenses as I got settled.

She was *an interesting woman* – a real piece of work. She had been through a lot in her life (and was still working through some of it), and had a reputation for being hard to deal with.

I wasn't too worried; I had confidence in my people skills. I had some training in negotiation and conflict management, and I was on a path of personal growth. I thought I could handle it. I told some friends that all I had to do was keep a dust buster in my back pocket and everything would be fine. We joked about it, and they even started calling me Mr. Dustbuster.

I soon found out I couldn't deal with her at all. It seemed like every time I turned around I broke another one of her household rules. She'd respond with a reprimand, or an angry outburst, or she'd leave me a nasty note about how rude and insensitive I was.

The rules were always changing. Whether it was putting something down where she didn't want it, parking my car where she wanted to drive, putting my food on the wrong shelf in the refrigerator, leaving a few unwashed dishes in the sink, putting a piece of food in the trash can instead of the compost bucket, opening the wrong door to let fresh air in, or not sweeping the floor in the right direction.

I've had bad experiences living with other people, but this was absolutely the worst. She was the most irascible person I had ever met.

I tried working things out with her. I knew she was working through stuff, but so was I. I bent over backwards to respect her space and her belongings and her privacy and her way of doing things, but she was completely inflexible in living with another human being.

I came home one evening, and as I pulled in the driveway, I looked up the hill towards the house. I could see her standing on the porch glaring down at me. *What is it this time?* I thought to myself, and then I did a double take. For what I saw in front of me was not the woman I was renting a room from. What I saw was an image of another woman from another time.

The woman I saw on the porch that day was my grandmother, my father's mother. Everything about her was the same: the defiant stance, the furrowed brow, the piercing gaze, the clenched jaw and tightened lips, the stiff neck, the tension in her forearms as she wiped her hands on her apron. All the same patterns of anger that I had experienced with my roommate matched up with the memories I had of my grandmother.

In that moment something clicked deep inside of me. I realized how angry my grandmother had been. My father, as her eldest son, had probably grown up receiving the brunt of her anger. I could appreciate what is must have been like to be raised by a cruel, controlling, cold-hearted bitch – a woman who was constantly critical, who never praised him, who never held him, and, in all likelihood emotionally abandoned him. I could see that my father never had a loving relationship with his mother. He had probably spent most of his life unconsciously seeking the feminine warmth he had been denied as a child.

After all these years, I understood my father as I never had before.

Forged Blades

Was thinking of my dad today. Random thoughts, memories, conversations – bitter and sweet. Found myself thinking about golf.

Dad loved to play golf. He was damn good at it. Could have played professionally. I never thought about that. Personally, I always thought his stories were a bit over the top. *I coulda' been a contender.* Still, he had the trophies, pictures, bag tags, and receipts. Memorabilia.

I love to play golf, too. Haven't played much lately, but I have memorabilia of my own: trophies, pictures, some damn good stories. I also have a special set of clubs that I keep tucked away.

The woods are real wood, carved from tight-grain persimmon, polished and laquered. The irons are real iron, heads made from carbon steel, forged and tempered, then chrome plated. Not the exact clubs my father played with, but from the time when he played. Years ago, I rebuilt this set. Each club, one by one. New grips, new chrome, new paint, new leather. A *period authentic* restoration.

The clubs are different makes and models, what you might call a mixed set. The putter is from Titleist, the woods from H&B, the bag and the irons from Wilson. The irons are stamped with the words *Tour Blade*. These are the clubs of a player.

To some, a blade is a weapon, a sword or a knife, the edges honed, the hilt curved to fit the hand, ready for the warrior to engage. It vibrates with energy when called into battle. *Schwing.*

To others, a blade is a tool, a precision instrument used to cut and slice and scrape. This blade is cold, sharp, unforgiving.

A blade can also be a structural member, slender and sleek. A shoulder blade. A propeller blade. A blade of grass.

Today, I cleaned and polished each club, one by one. And I thought about my dad.

My dad never coached me in the game of golf. He never gave me lessons, never offered advice, never said I was wrong, never helped me get it right.

Today, I realized that golf was one of the few things in life where he never criticized me. He never criticized my grip, my stance, my swing, my approach to the game.

He let me play my own game.

Knives

I've always been afraid of knives. Some people are afraid of guns. I've always had a healthy respect for guns, but I've never been afraid of them. My dad was a hunter, as were all of the men on his side of the family, and a gun was a tool for hunting. It was a tool to be cared for, taken care of, and used responsibly.

Somehow a knife was different, and dangerous.

I remember working on a model car, a kit with all the parts molded out of plastic. I don't remember the model, but it was a sports car, and the hood had an option where you could cut out a hole and let the engine pipes stick up. I thought it would look cool.

I grabbed a knife and started cutting. At some point, my finger got in the way. I saw the blood first, then felt the pain. I remember screaming, shaking my hand like a rag doll, blood dripping and flying everywhere, the floor, the walls, the ceiling.

I had almost severed the tip of the index finger on my left hand. My mother calmed me down, put me in bed, and cleaned up the blood.

A few hours later, my father came home. I remember them talking quietly, about taking me to the emergency room, to get stitches. I didn't want to go. I was crying and shaking. I can still hear my father's voice. *He's in shock.*

Years later, I was using the blade of my boy scout knife as a screw driver. It was a folding pen knife, without the locking mechanism to keep the blade secure, like they have today.

It was a stupid thing to do. As I pushed and turned, the blade collapsed on my finger, cutting the knuckle of my pointing finger down to the bone. This time, I got stitches. It took months to heal. It still clicks whenever I bend my finger.

So yeah, I have some scars from knives. But I think my fear of knives cuts deeper than that.

I can remember my parents standing in the family room, screaming at each other. Another fight about who knows what. My mother on one side, my father on the other. Anger in their voices, and in their eyes. My father with a butcher knife in his hand.

I think my father struck first. Only they didn't strike each other, they struck at things that were dear to the other.

My mother loved to knit. She made throws and sweaters, and decorative things. I think they call it macrame. My father grabbed one of her hanging planters, cut the cords with the knife, and slammed it on the floor. My mother screamed, and then quickly struck back.

My father had a small shrine made of wood, with seven lucky gods carved out of small pieces of ivory. A memento he had brought home from Japan, after being stationed there. I remember my mother grabbing the shrine, lifting it over her head, and smashing it on the floor. I remember the sound of the wood cracking and splintering, and watching the carved pieces of ivory as they danced across the floor. Seven little gods, lucky no more.

I think that's why I am afraid of knives.

Birds and Bees

"Dad, what's an orgasm?"

Just kidding. I never asked my father that question. In fact, my father and I never talked about sex. Never.

There were lots of things we never discussed. But sex was one thing that we *avoided* completely.

I don't know exactly why. I am sure part of it was the zeitgeist. People just didn't talk about those things back then.

You'll know what to do when the time comes.

Like most boys, my sex education happened at school. Not in classes, but in the locker room, on the playground, in the cafeteria. Places of research and learning, in quiet conversations with people *who knew*.

My mother gave me a booklet when I was twelve or so. It had details about human reproduction - the birds and the bees. I remember reading it cover to cover at one sitting. I was fascinated. Nervous. Aroused.

When I was finished, she asked if I had any questions.

Ahhh, no. I'm good.

My mother and I never talked about sex after that, although she made it obvious that anything to do with sex was sinful and disgusting.

My father and I never talked about sex either, other than to identify the gender in various animals. A bull. A cow. A stallion. A mare. A hen. A cock. Funny how that word has so much energy around it.

In biology class, I learned about eggs and sperm and gametes. RNA and DNA and genetics. Animal migrations. Breeding seasons. Gestation periods.

So, as I entered my teens, I wasn't completely ignorant about sex, but I had no idea what it really meant.

I wish my father had talked to me, one on one, on what was about to happen. What a wild ride I was in for. It would have made my life so much easier.

"Son, when you get older, some things are going to happen to your body. For starters, you are going to grow hair in places you never expected. Don't worry, it's not that big a deal.

You are going to have dreams. Weird dreams. Crazy dreams. Sexy dreams. And you're going to wet the bed.

It's a different kind of wetting the bed. And way more fun. Keep a spare pair of pajamas near by, and a wash cloth."

But he never said that. He never told me what was going to happen. Never told me what I should do.

Instead, I had quiet conversations with the boys at school. They were wise and experienced in the mysteries of sex. And they gave me such useful advice.

Not.

"Son, you remember that fishing trip to Canada, when we saw that crumpled car that had hit a moose? That wasn't a moose running across the road. That moose ran into that car, head on, intentionally. During what we call a mating rut. It's triggered by hormones and pheromones and weather patterns and god knows what.

When you get older, that same thing is going to happen to you. It might be triggered by something you see, something you smell, something you eat, something in the air, or a combination of things.

But when it happens, things are going to spin out of control. Your heart will start racing, and you are going to be dizzy and disoriented. You won't be able to think straight. You won't be able to see straight. You are going to want one thing, and one thing only, and that's the only thing that is going to matter."

But he never said that either. He never told me what a mating rut was going to be like. Never told me how to deal with it. Never told me what I should do.

Perhaps if he had, I wouldn't have felt so guilty and embarassed about what started happening to me. Or the things that I did when I was alone, or thought no one was looking.

If only we had been able to talk about things, one on one. The kind of relationship where I could have asked him a simple question.

"Dad, what's an orgasm?"

Son, an orgasm is something out of this world. It is something to enjoy, to celebrate, even to die for.

Right now, you're too young to understand all this, but soon, your body is going to start changing, in ways magical and confusing. Your body will be able to experience orgasm, and you are going to be dealing with the pursuit of orgasm for the rest of your life.

It's hard to explain, exactly, but here are some things to consider . . .

Diamonds

I remember the last time I saw my father, in the spring of 2011. An F5 tornado had touched down in Tuscaloosa, Alabama, a few miles from where he lived. I was on a plane a few days later.

My dad and stepmother were unhurt, but my stepsister and her family were in the thick of things. Their house was standing, surrounded by fallen trees. A block away, devastation everywhere. Houses crushed – or gone – the house next door untouched. Rubble everywhere, cement blocks and bricks and broken glass, tree trunks scattered like broken toothpicks. On the ground in front of me, a paperback book, with the cover missing. Pieces of people's homes. Lives torn apart.

For three days we sorted through debris, surrounded by the sights and sounds of a disaster zone. Police at every intersection. A symphony of helicopters, trucks, bulldozers, and chainsaws. Then nightfall, curfew, and everything quiet until dawn.

In those three days, I learned more about Alabama than I had in the previous three decades. They were amazing people. Strong, proud, independent. People I never really knew before. In a place my father had come to call home.

I remember driving back to my dad's house the first day. I don't think I've ever been that tired. I remember taking a long, hot shower, and plopping into a chair in the living room. My dad lying on the couch, watching TV.

We chatted for a bit. As usual, he started bitchin' and moaning about something, everything. I wasn't in the mood. I got up, and started searching for a refreshing adult beverage. On my way back, I noticed the prescription bottles on the bathroom countertop. Brown bottles and white lids, spread out like cattle on the back forty. My dad had been in poor health for years. Surgeries, stents, procedures, most of them invasive. He was often in pain.

Hmmm, maybe there is something in here I could use.

I came back to the living room, plopped down, and put my feet up. The door to the patio was open. The sun was sparkling off the water. Diamonds dancing on the waves.

A warm glow slowly spread over me, through me. I couldn't hear what my dad was saying, didn't really care. I was simply glad to be there.

It was just me and my dad, hanging out on a warm spring day.

The way I always wanted it to be.

A Knock on My Door

I left home years ago
to make my way in the world
'twas four decades and more

I was young and proud
college bound
the first of my kind
to dare and to climb

on graduation day
my family stayed home
it's too far, too cold, and we're busy you know
you're right I said. even I did not go

magna cum laude
the diploma said
it's in a drawer somewhere
unseen and unread

I set forth that day
to make my way
smart and well trained
how hard could it be?

along the way
I often stumbled and fell
felt his fury on the phone
at my stupidity

over time I got . . . settled
made a house and a home
I started waiting
for a knock on my door

my sister knocked once
some decades ago
my mother twice, perhaps thrice
my younger brother as well

still I kept waiting
for a knock on my door

my father loved to travel
with his new wife and new life
Las Vegas. Bermuda. Aruba. Cancun.
I kept thinking he would visit
one day soon

there were time zones to consider
expensive airfare
commitments and deadlines
dogs that need care

still I kept waiting
for a knock on my door

he thought about it. talked about it.
once even made plans
but something came up
it was out of his hands

still I kept waiting
for a knock on my door

It's so far and so hard
my health is no good
I can't travel alone
and I understood

still I kept waiting
for a knock on my door

politicians kiss babies
pose for photos and smile
they talk about family
to cultivate votes

blood may be thicker than water
but that doesn't explain
why the people you love
can hurt you the most

forever waiting
for a knock on my door

The End

Epilogue

In Memory of Roger Larson

born: Nov 14, 1930

died: Feb 17, 2018

www.ingramcontent.com/pod-product-compliance
Lightning Source LLC
Chambersburg PA
CBHW070439100426
42812CB00031B/3341/J